MW01071637

YOUR COMPLETE SAGITTARIUS 2025 PERSONAL HOROSCOPE

Monthly Astrological Prediction Forecast Readings of Every Zodiac Astrology Sun Star Signs- Love, Romance, Money, Finances, Career, Health, Travel, Spirituality.

Iris Quinn

Alpha Zuriel Publishing

Your Complete Sagittarius 2025 Personal Horoscope/ Iris Quinn. -- 1st ed.

"Astrology is a language. If you understand this language, the sky speaks to you."
— IRIS QUINN

CONTENTS

CHAPTER ONE

SAGITTARIUS PROFILE

General Characteristics

- **Element:** Fire
- **Quality:** Mutable
- **Ruler:** Jupiter
- **Symbol:** The Archer
- **Dates:** November 22 - December 21

Personality Traits

- **Adventurous:** Loves exploring new places and ideas.
- **Optimistic:** Maintains a positive outlook on life.
- **Independent:** Values freedom and self-reliance.
- **Philosophical:** Enjoys pondering deep questions and exploring various philosophies.
- **Honest:** Known for being straightforward and candid.
- **Generous:** Willingly shares time, resources, and affection with others.

- **Curious:** Possesses a strong desire to learn and experience new things.
- **Energetic:** Full of vitality and enthusiasm.
- **Visionary:** Always looking towards the future with big ideas.
- **Impatient:** Can be restless and eager for quick results.

Strengths

- **Optimism:** Inspires others with their positive attitude.
- **Adventurous Spirit:** Thrives on new experiences and exploration.
- **Generosity:** Open-hearted and giving to those around them.
- **Honesty:** Values truth and integrity in all interactions.
- **Curiosity:** Constantly seeks knowledge and understanding.
- **Enthusiasm:** Brings energy and excitement to their endeavors.
- **Visionary Thinking:** Sees possibilities and potentials that others might overlook.

Weaknesses

- **Impatience:** Often wants immediate results and can become frustrated with delays.
- **Restlessness:** Struggles with staying in one place or situation for too long.
- **Tactlessness:** Honesty can sometimes be blunt and hurtful.

- **Overconfidence:** Can overestimate their abilities or luck.
- **Inconsistency:** May struggle with following through on long-term commitments.
- **Escapism:** Sometimes avoids responsibilities or uncomfortable situations.

Planets and Their Influences

- **Career Planet:** Saturn – Provides discipline and structure in professional life.
- **Love Planet:** Venus – Governs affection and relationships.
- **Money Planet:** Jupiter – Rules financial matters and abundance.
- **Planet of Fun, Entertainment, Creativity, and Speculations:** Jupiter – Encourages optimism and joy.
- **Planet of Health and Work:** Mercury – Influences communication and routine.
- **Planet of Home and Family Life:** Moon – Governs emotions and domestic affairs.
- **Planet of Spirituality:** Neptune – Represents dreams and intuition.
- **Planet of Travel, Education, Religion, and Philosophy:** Jupiter – Governs expansion and learning.

Compatibility

- **Signs of Greatest Overall Compatibility:** Aries, Leo
- **Signs of Greatest Overall Incompatibility:** Virgo, Pisces

- **Sign Most Supportive for Career Advancement:** Capricorn
- **Sign Most Supportive for Emotional Well-being:** Aries
- **Sign Most Supportive Financially:** Taurus
- **Sign Best for Marriage and/or Partnerships:** Gemini
- **Sign Most Supportive for Creative Projects:** Leo
- **Best Sign to Have Fun With:** Sagittarius
- **Signs Most Supportive in Spiritual Matters:** Pisces
- **Best Day of the Week:** Thursday

Additional Details

- **Colors:** Purple, Royal Blue
- **Gem:** Turquoise
- **Scent:** Clove, Cinnamon
- **Birthstone:** Turquoise
- **Quality:** Mutable (adaptable and flexible)

PERSONALITY OF SAGITTARIUS

Sagittarius, born between November 22 and December 21, is a fire sign ruled by Jupiter, the planet of expansion, optimism, and abundance. This combination gives Sagittarians a personality that is vibrant, adventurous, and perpetually optimistic. They are known for their insatiable curiosity and love for exploration, both of the physical world and the realm of ideas. This sign embodies a free spirit, always seeking new experiences and knowledge, making them one of the most dynamic and forward-thinking signs of the zodiac.

At the heart of a Sagittarius' personality is their adventurous nature. They are drawn to new horizons and thrive on the excitement of discovery. Whether it's traveling to distant lands, delving into different cultures, or exploring new philosophies, Sagittarians have an innate desire to broaden their understanding and experience of the world. This adventurous spirit is not just limited to physical travel; they also enjoy intellectual pursuits, constantly seeking to expand their minds with new ideas and perspectives.

Sagittarians are known for their boundless optimism. They have a positive outlook on life and are often seen as the eternal optimists of the zodiac. This optimism can be infectious, as they have a way of lifting the spirits of those around them. They believe in the best possible outcomes and have a knack for finding the silver lining in any situation. This positive mindset helps them to navigate challenges with resilience and grace, always looking forward to the next adventure with enthusiasm.

Independence is another key trait of Sagittarius. They value their freedom highly and often resist anything that feels restrictive or confining. This need for independence is reflected in their approach to life and relationships. They prefer to carve their own path and make their own decisions, often rebelling against societal norms and expectations. While this can sometimes make them appear rebellious or nonconformist, it is simply their way of staying true to their authentic selves.

Sagittarians are also incredibly honest and straightforward. They believe in speaking their mind and value truth above all else. This honesty can sometimes come across as bluntness, as they are not ones to sugarcoat their opinions. While their candor is appreciated by those who value transparency, it can occasionally lead to misunderstandings or hurt feelings. However, Sagittarians' intentions are rarely malicious; they simply believe in the importance of being genuine and open.

Generosity is another hallmark of the Sagittarius personality. They are open-hearted and giving, always willing to lend a hand or share their resources with those in need. This generosity extends to their time and attention as well, as they are genuinely interested in the well-being of others. Their willingness to share their knowledge, experiences, and even material possessions makes them beloved friends and partners.

Despite their many strengths, Sagittarians can sometimes struggle with consistency and follow-through. Their enthusiasm for new projects and ideas can lead to a tendency to start many things but finish few. They may become easily bored or restless, always seeking the next exciting opportunity. This restlessness can sometimes be mistaken for a lack of commitment, but it is more a reflection of their desire to experience as much as possible in life.

Sagittarians are also known for their visionary thinking. They are big-picture thinkers who are always looking towards the future. This visionary quality allows them to see possibilities and potentials that others might overlook. However, it can also mean that they sometimes overlook the details or the practicalities of bringing their visions to life. They thrive in environments that allow them to dream big and think creatively, often inspiring those around them to do the same.

In relationships, Sagittarians are passionate and open-hearted. They seek partners who share their love for adventure and their zest for life. They value intellectual stimulation and appreciate partners who can engage them in deep, meaningful conversations. While they cherish their independence, they are also deeply loyal and committed to those they love. They need partners who can give them the freedom they crave while also providing a sense of stability and support.

In conclusion, the personality of Sagittarius is a blend of adventure, optimism, independence, and generosity. They are driven by a desire to explore and understand the world, both physically and intellectually. Their honest and straightforward nature, combined with their boundless enthusiasm and visionary thinking, makes them inspiring and dynamic individuals. While their need for freedom and occasional restlessness can pose challenges, their ability to see the big picture and their generous spirit make them invaluable companions on the journey of life.

WEAKNESSES OF SAGITTARIUS

As an astrologer, delving into the weaknesses of Sagittarius, it becomes clear that their strengths often have a flip side that can present challenges. Sagittarius, ruled by Jupiter and known for their boundless enthusiasm and love for adventure, can sometimes find themselves grappling with certain traits that complicate their lives and relationships.

One of the primary weaknesses of Sagittarius is their tendency towards restlessness. Their insatiable curiosity and desire for new experiences, while invigorating, can also make them prone to boredom. They often struggle with staying in one place or sticking to one project for too long. This restlessness can lead to a pattern of starting many endeavors but finishing few, as the excitement of the new often overshadows the commitment required to see things through to completion. This trait can affect their personal and professional lives, causing frustration for themselves and those who rely on their consistency.

Sagittarius' love for freedom and independence, while admirable, can sometimes morph into a fear of commitment. They cherish their autonomy and can become uncomfortable when they feel their freedom is being threatened. In relationships, this can manifest as an aversion to long-term commitments or a reluctance to settle down. Their partners might find it challenging to understand this need for space, interpreting it as a lack of interest or dedication. It is crucial for Sagittarians to communicate their needs clearly and find a balance between their independence and their commitment to loved ones.

Their honesty, often seen as a virtue, can also be a double-edged sword. Sagittarians are known for their straightforwardness and their refusal to sugarcoat the truth. While this candor is appreciated for its transparency, it can sometimes come across as tactlessness. They might unintentionally hurt others' feelings by being too blunt or insensitive, failing to consider the impact of their words. Developing a sense of empathy and learning to deliver their honesty with more sensitivity can help mitigate this issue.

Overconfidence is another trait that can occasionally work against Sagittarius. Their optimism and belief in their abilities can sometimes lead to overestimating what they can achieve or taking on more than they can handle. This overconfidence can result in taking unnecessary risks or making promises they cannot keep. It can also cause them to overlook important details, as they are often focused on the big picture. Learning to temper their enthusiasm with a bit of caution and humility can help them avoid potential pitfalls.

Inconsistency is a challenge for many Sagittarians. Their enthusiasm for new ideas and ventures can wane as quickly as it begins, leading to a lack of follow-through. This inconsistency can frustrate their colleagues and partners, who may find it difficult to depend on them for sustained effort or support. Recognizing this tendency and working on strategies to maintain their focus and commitment can help Sagittarians achieve more balanced and reliable outcomes.

Finally, escapism is a weakness that Sagittarians might encounter. Their desire for adventure and new experiences can sometimes turn into a means of avoiding responsibilities or uncomfortable situations. When faced with difficulties, they might prefer to escape into their next adventure rather than dealing with the problem at hand. This avoidance can lead to unresolved issues piling up, creating more significant challenges in the long run. Learning to face their problems directly and finding healthy ways to cope with stress can help them overcome this tendency.

In essence, while Sagittarius possesses many admirable qualities, their weaknesses often stem from the very traits that make them unique. Their restlessness, fear of commitment, blunt honesty, overconfidence, inconsistency, and tendency towards escapism are challenges that they must navigate. By acknowledging these weaknesses and working towards balancing their natural inclinations with more mindful and considerate behavior, Sagittarians can harness their strengths while mitigating the impact of their less favorable traits. This journey of self-awareness and growth can lead to a more fulfilling and harmonious life for themselves and those around them.

RELATIONSHIP COMPATIBILITY WITH SAGITTARIUS

Based only on their Sun signs, this is how Sagittarius interacts with others. These are the compatibility interpretations for all 12 potential Sagittarius combinations. This is a limited and insufficient method of determining compatibility.

However, Sun-sign compatibility remains the foundation for overall harmony in a relationship.

The general rule is that yin and yang do not get along. Yin complements yin, and yang complements yang. While yin and yang partnerships can be successful, they require more effort. Earth and water zodiac signs are both Yin. Yang is represented by the fire and air zodiac signs.

Sagittarius with Yang Signs (Fire and Air)

Sagittarius and Aries (Yang with Yang):

When Sagittarius and Aries come together, the relationship is filled with excitement, energy, and

14

adventure. Both partners share a love for exploration and new experiences, making their union dynamic and constantly evolving. They understand each other's need for independence and freedom, which helps them avoid feelings of restriction. Their mutual optimism and enthusiasm can lead to a fun and vibrant relationship, although their tendency to be impulsive and sometimes blunt can lead to occasional conflicts. To make this relationship work, they need to balance their adventurous spirits with a bit of patience and understanding.

Sagittarius and Leo (Yang with Yang):

Sagittarius and Leo form a passionate and charismatic pair. Both signs are adventurous, energetic, and enjoy being in the spotlight. Leo's confidence and charisma complement Sagittarius' optimism and sense of adventure. They inspire each other and have a strong mutual admiration. However, their strong personalities can sometimes clash, leading to power struggles. To avoid conflicts, they need to practice compromise and ensure that their competitive streaks do not overshadow their mutual respect and love. Communication and understanding are key to maintaining harmony in this vibrant relationship.

Sagittarius and Sagittarius (Yang with Yang):

When two Sagittarians come together, the relationship is characterized by a mutual love for adventure, freedom, and philosophical exploration. They share a similar outlook on life and enjoy discovering new experiences together. This pairing can be highly stimulating and exciting, as both partners encourage each other's growth and independence. However, their mutual need for freedom can sometimes lead to a lack of stability and commitment. To make this relationship work, they need to find a balance between their adventurous spirits and the need for a stable and grounded partnership.

Sagittarius and Gemini (Yang with Yang):

The relationship between Sagittarius and Gemini is lively and intellectually stimulating. Gemini's curiosity and adaptability complement Sagittarius' enthusiasm and love for adventure. They enjoy a mentally engaging partnership where boredom rarely sets in, thanks to Gemini's versatile nature and Sagittarius' drive for exploration. Sagittarius can sometimes be frustrated by Gemini's indecisiveness, while Gemini may find Sagittarius too impulsive. To make this pairing work, they need to appreciate each

16

other's strengths—Gemini's communicative skills and Sagittarius' decisiveness—and find a balance between flexibility and action.

Sagittarius and Libra (Yang with Yang):

Sagittarius and Libra create a dynamic and balanced relationship. Libra's charm, diplomacy, and love for harmony complement Sagittarius' adventurous spirit and philosophical nature. Libra can help Sagittarius see different perspectives and create balance, while Sagittarius adds excitement and initiative to Libra's life. Their relationship thrives on mutual admiration and a shared love for new experiences. However, Sagittarius' directness can sometimes clash with Libra's desire for peace, leading to occasional conflicts. Communication and understanding are essential for maintaining harmony. By learning to appreciate their differences, they can create a harmonious and fulfilling partnership.

Sagittarius and Aquarius (Yang with Yang):

Sagittarius and Aquarius share a love for independence, innovation, and intellectual exploration. Aquarius' visionary ideas and unconventional approach to life attract Sagittarius, who admires their originality and intellect. Sagittarius' enthusiasm and action-oriented nature inspire Aquarius, creating a relationship that is both exciting and intellectually stimulating. They enjoy exploring new ideas and experiences together, keeping their relationship fresh and dynamic. However, both signs value their freedom, which can sometimes lead to a lack of emotional closeness. They need to work on maintaining a strong emotional connection while respecting each other's need for independence.

Sagittarius with Yin Signs (Earth and Water)

Sagittarius and Taurus (Yang with Yin):

Sagittarius and Taurus have contrasting energies that can make their relationship challenging but rewarding. Sagittarius is spontaneous and adventurous, while Taurus is steady, practical, and values security. Sagittarius can bring excitement and a sense of adventure to Taurus's life, encouraging them to step out of their comfort zone. Conversely, Taurus can offer Sagittarius stability and patience, helping them to slow down and appreciate the finer details of life. For this relationship to work, both partners need to be willing to understand and appreciate their differences.

Sagittarius should be more considerate of Taurus's need for stability and routine, while Taurus should be open to change and new experiences. Communication and mutual respect are crucial for creating a balanced and enriching partnership.

Sagittarius and Virgo (Yang with Yin):

Sagittarius and Virgo have very different approaches to life, which can create friction but also offer opportunities for growth. Sagittarius is impulsive, action-oriented, and loves taking risks, while Virgo is analytical, methodical, and prefers careful planning. Sagittarius might find Virgo's attention to detail and cautious nature frustrating, while Virgo might see Sagittarius as reckless and inconsiderate. However, if they can learn from each other, this relationship can be complementary. Sagittarius can benefit from Virgo's organizational skills and practical approach, while Virgo can be inspired by Sagittarius' boldness and willingness to take risks. Patience, understanding, and a willingness to compromise are essential for making this pairing work.

Sagittarius and Capricorn (Yang with Yin):

Sagittarius and Capricorn have a challenging yet potentially rewarding relationship. Sagittarius is spontaneous and seeks immediate results, while Capricorn is disciplined, focused on long-term goals, and prefers a structured approach. These differing outlooks can lead to misunderstandings and conflicts. However, if they can appreciate each other's strengths, they can form a powerful team. Sagittarius can bring energy and enthusiasm to Capricorn's plans, injecting a sense of urgency and excitement. Conversely, Capricorn can provide the structure and persistence that Sagittarius needs to achieve their goals. This relationship requires patience, compromise, and a willingness to understand each other's perspectives. When they work together, they can achieve great things.

Sagittarius and Cancer (Yang with Yin):

Sagittarius and Cancer have contrasting needs and approaches that can make their relationship challenging but potentially very rewarding. Sagittarius is independent, adventurous, and often focuses on their own goals, while Cancer is sensitive, nurturing, and seeks emotional connection and security. Sagittarius can sometimes be too direct and forceful for Cancer's delicate nature, leading to hurt feelings. However, if they learn to appreciate each other's differences, they can form a complementary partnership. Sagittarius can bring excitement and courage to Cancer's life, encouraging them to step out of their emotional comfort zone. In return, Cancer can provide emotional support and care, teaching Sagittarius the value of empathy and nurturing. Mutual understanding and respect are essential to making this relationship work.

Sagittarius and Scorpio (Yang with Yin):

Sagittarius and Scorpio have a relationship filled with intensity and passion. Both signs are strong-willed, determined, and possess a deep emotional connection, which can create a powerful and transformative bond. Sagittarius is drawn to Scorpio's mysterious and intense nature, while Scorpio appreciates Sagittarius' courage and straightforwardness. However, their mutual desire for control and independence can lead to power struggles and conflicts. To make this relationship work, they need to be mindful of their tempers, learn to compromise, and respect each other's strengths. When they work together, they can achieve great things and create a deeply fulfilling and passionate relationship.

Sagittarius and Pisces (Yang with Yin):

Sagittarius and Pisces have very different natures that can make their relationship challenging but potentially rewarding. Sagittarius is bold, adventurous, and action-oriented, while Pisces is gentle, introspective, and driven by their emotions. Sagittarius can sometimes be too aggressive or blunt for Pisces' sensitive nature, leading to misunderstandings and hurt feelings. However, if they learn to appreciate each other's differences, they can form a complementary partnership. Sagittarius can help Pisces be more confident and assertive, encouraging them to pursue their dreams actively. In return, Pisces can teach Sagittarius about compassion, creativity, and the value of emotional connection. This relationship requires patience, understanding, and a willingness to learn from each other.

In conclusion, Sagittarius' compatibility with other sun signs varies widely based on the yin and yang theory. Fire and air signs generally complement Sagittarius' energetic and adventurous nature, leading to vibrant and exciting relationships. Earth and water signs, while presenting more challenges, can provide balance and stability, requiring more effort to navigate their differences. With mutual respect, understanding, and a willingness to learn from each other, Sagittarius can form successful and fulfilling partnerships with any sign.

LOVE AND PASSION

Love and passion for Sagittarius are intense, vibrant, and deeply intertwined with their innate sense of adventure and curiosity. Ruled by Jupiter, the planet of expansion and growth, Sagittarius approaches love with an enthusiasm that is both contagious and exhilarating. They are eternal seekers, always looking for new experiences and deeper understanding, and this quest naturally extends to their romantic relationships.

In love, Sagittarius is driven by a profound need for freedom and independence. They value partners who understand their need for space and who can match their enthusiasm for life's adventures. This sign thrives on spontaneity and excitement, and they are always eager to explore new horizons with their loved ones. Whether it's planning impromptu trips, trying out new activities, or engaging in deep, philosophical conversations, Sagittarius is always looking to expand their experiences and grow alongside their partner.

Passion for Sagittarius is not merely a physical expression but a full engagement of their mind, body, and spirit. They are highly sensual beings who enjoy exploring the depths of physical intimacy. However, their passion goes beyond the physical realm; it is deeply intellectual and emotional as well. They are attracted to partners who can stimulate their minds and engage them in meaningful conversations. For Sagittarius, mental connection is just as important as physical attraction, and they seek partners who can challenge and inspire them.

One of the most captivating aspects of a Sagittarius lover is their optimism and positivity. They have an infectious enthusiasm that can light up any room, and they bring this same energy into their relationships. They believe in the best possible outcomes and are always looking for ways to make their partner's life more joyful and fulfilling. This positive outlook helps them to navigate the ups and downs of relationships with grace and resilience, always looking for the silver lining in any situation.

However, the Sagittarian need for freedom and adventure can sometimes pose challenges in relationships. They can be wary of commitment if they feel it might restrict their independence. It is crucial for their partners to understand this aspect of their personality and to give them the space they need to explore and grow. Trust and mutual respect are essential in maintaining a healthy relationship with a

Sagittarius. They need to feel that their partner supports their need for independence while also being a steady and reliable presence in their lives.

Sagittarians are also known for their honesty and straightforwardness. They value truth and integrity and expect the same from their partners. This honesty, while refreshing, can sometimes come across as bluntness, as Sagittarius is not one to sugarcoat their thoughts or feelings. It is important for their partners to appreciate this trait and understand that their directness comes from a place of genuine care and desire for transparency.

Despite their independent nature, Sagittarius is deeply loyal and devoted once they commit to a relationship. They are passionate about their loved ones and will go to great lengths to support and protect them. Their generosity knows no bounds, and they are always willing to share their time, resources, and affection with those they care about. This loyalty creates a strong foundation for their relationships, providing their partners with a sense of security and unwavering support.

Sagittarius is also incredibly adaptable and open-minded. They are always willing to try new things and embrace change, which can make their relationships dynamic and ever-evolving. They are not afraid to take risks and often encourage their partners to step out of their comfort zones. This willingness to embrace the unknown and take on new challenges together can create a deeply enriching and fulfilling partnership.

In summary, love and passion for Sagittarius are characterized by a blend of adventure, intellectual curiosity, and a deep desire for growth and expansion. They seek partners who can match their enthusiasm for life and who understand their need for freedom and independence. Their relationships are marked by honesty, loyalty, and a sense of excitement and exploration. While their straightforwardness and desire for independence can sometimes pose challenges, their optimistic and generous nature makes them deeply loving and devoted partners. Through mutual respect, open communication, and a shared sense of adventure, Sagittarius can create passionate and enduring relationships that are as dynamic as they are fulfilling.

MARRIAGE

Marriage for Sagittarius is a dynamic journey filled with adventure, exploration, and growth. Ruled by Jupiter, the planet of expansion and optimism, Sagittarians bring a unique energy to their marital relationships. Their inherent love for freedom and independence shapes their approach to marriage, making it essential to understand and embrace their need for space and adventure to keep them happy and fulfilled in this lifelong commitment.

To keep a Sagittarius happy in marriage, it is crucial to foster an environment that respects and nurtures their sense of independence. They thrive in relationships where their need for personal freedom is understood and supported. This means allowing them the space to pursue their interests, hobbies, and adventures without feeling confined or restricted. Encouraging their explorative spirit can strengthen the bond, as they appreciate partners who share their enthusiasm for life and are willing to embark on new journeys together.

Sagittarius men in marriage are vibrant, enthusiastic, and deeply committed to personal growth and discovery. They bring a sense of excitement and optimism to the relationship, often inspiring their partners to embrace new experiences and perspectives. A Sagittarius man values honesty and openness, and he expects the same from his partner. He thrives in an environment where communication is straightforward and transparent, allowing both partners to express their needs and desires freely. To keep a Sagittarius man happy, it is important to engage in activities that stimulate his mind and spirit, such as traveling, exploring new cultures, or engaging in intellectual discussions. His adventurous nature makes him an exciting and passionate partner, always eager to explore new dimensions of life and love.

Sagittarius women in marriage are equally passionate and adventurous. They bring a zest for life and a strong sense of independence to their relationships. A Sagittarius woman values a partner who is not only supportive but also willing to grow and evolve alongside her. She seeks a relationship that is built on mutual respect and shared interests. To keep a Sagittarius woman happy, it is essential to embrace her need for freedom and encourage her to pursue her passions. She appreciates a partner who is open-minded and willing to explore new horizons, whether through travel, learning new skills, or engaging in creative pursuits. Her enthusiasm and optimism are contagious, making her a lively and inspiring partner.

The secret to making a marriage with Sagittarius work lies in balancing their need for independence with a strong sense of partnership. Trust and mutual respect are the cornerstones of a successful marriage with Sagittarius. They need to feel that their partner trusts them and respects their individuality. This trust fosters a deeper connection, allowing both partners to feel secure and valued in the relationship. Open communication is also essential, as Sagittarians value honesty and transparency. Being able to express thoughts, feelings, and concerns openly helps to maintain a healthy and harmonious relationship.

Adventure and novelty are vital elements in keeping the spark alive in a marriage with Sagittarius. They thrive on new experiences and love to explore the unknown. Planning spontaneous trips, trying out new activities, or simply breaking the routine can keep the relationship exciting and dynamic. Sagittarians appreciate partners who share their love for adventure and are willing to step out of their comfort zones. This shared sense of adventure not only strengthens the bond but also creates lasting memories that enrich the relationship.

Another key aspect of a successful marriage with Sagittarius is maintaining a sense of individuality within the partnership. While they are deeply loyal and committed, Sagittarians need to feel that they have their own identity and personal space. Encouraging each other to pursue individual interests and passions can enhance the relationship, as it allows both partners to grow and evolve independently while also supporting each other's journeys.

Understanding and embracing the philosophical and intellectual nature of Sagittarius can also enhance the marital bond. They are naturally curious and love to engage in deep, meaningful conversations. Sharing ideas, discussing different perspectives, and exploring philosophical questions can create a strong intellectual connection, which is highly valued by Sagittarians. This intellectual stimulation can deepen the emotional bond and foster a sense of mutual respect and admiration.

In summary, marriage for Sagittarius is a blend of adventure, independence, and intellectual exploration. Keeping a Sagittarius happy in marriage requires understanding and respecting their need for freedom, encouraging their sense of adventure, and fostering open and honest communication. Whether male or female, Sagittarians bring a vibrant and enthusiastic energy to their relationships, making them dynamic and inspiring partners. By balancing their need for independence with a strong sense of partnership, maintaining trust and mutual respect, and embracing their love for novelty and intellectual engagement, a marriage with Sagittarius can be deeply fulfilling and enduring.

CHAPTER TWO

SAGITTARIUS 2025 HOROSCOPE

Overview Sagittarius 2025

Sagittarius (November 22 - December 21)

2025 is a year of expansion, adventure, and personal growth for those born under the sign of Sagittarius. The celestial bodies will align to bring you opportunities to broaden your horizons, explore new frontiers, and discover your true potential. Embrace the journey with an open mind and a curious heart, and trust that the universe has your back.

The year begins with Jupiter, your ruling planet, in the sign of Gemini. This placement suggests a strong focus on learning, communication, and intellectual pursuits in the first part of the year. You may find yourself drawn to new ideas, perspectives, and experiences that challenge your beliefs and expand your mind. This is a time to feed your curiosity, to engage in stimulating conversations, and to seek out knowledge and wisdom wherever you can find it.

In early February, Jupiter will turn direct in your 7th house of partnerships, bringing a renewed sense of optimism and growth to your closest relationships. This is a time to deepen your connections with others, to seek out new collaborations and alliances, and to learn from the people around you. Be open to the insights and perspectives of others, and trust that the right people will come into your life at the right time.

As the year progresses, a significant shift occurs in April when Pluto turns retrograde in your 3rd house of communication and learning. This transit may bring up deep-seated fears or insecurities around your ability to express yourself and be heard. It's a time to confront any limiting beliefs or patterns that may be holding you back from speaking your truth and sharing your ideas with the world. Trust in the power of your voice and your unique perspective, and know that your words have the power to inspire and transform.

The Total Lunar Eclipse in Pisces on September 7 will bring a powerful opportunity for emotional healing and spiritual growth. This eclipse falls in your 4th house of home and family, highlighting the need for a strong foundation and a sense of belonging. It's a time to let go of any past wounds or traumas that may be holding you back, and to embrace a deeper sense of love, compassion, and understanding for yourself and your loved ones. Trust in the power of forgiveness and release, and know that you are worthy of the love and support you seek.

In mid-June, Saturn will briefly shift into Aries, activating your 5th house of creativity, self-expression, and romance. This transit may bring some challenges or obstacles to your creative pursuits or your love life, but it's also an opportunity to build a stronger foundation for long-term success and fulfillment. Focus on developing your skills, your discipline, and your commitment to your passions, and trust that your efforts will pay off in the long run.

The second half of the year brings a focus on career, public image, and personal achievement. Mars, the planet of action and ambition, will spend an extended period in your 10th house of career and public recognition, bringing a powerful drive and determination to succeed. This is a time to take bold action towards your goals, to assert your leadership and authority, and to make your mark on the world. Trust in your abilities and your unique talents, and know that you have what it takes to achieve your dreams.

In late October, Jupiter will turn retrograde in your 8th house of transformation and shared resources, bringing a period of reflection and re-evaluation around your deepest fears, desires, and motivations. This is a time to confront any shadows or hidden aspects of yourself that may be holding you back from true intimacy and connection with others. It's also an opportunity to reassess your financial situation and your relationship with money and resources. Trust in the power of honesty, vulnerability, and self-awareness, and know that the challenges you face are ultimately serving your highest growth and evolution.

As the year comes to a close, the Partial Solar Eclipse in Sagittarius on December 19 will bring a powerful opportunity for new beginnings and fresh starts. This eclipse falls in your 1st house of self and identity, highlighting the need for authentic self-expression and personal autonomy. It's a time to let go of any masks or facades you may have been wearing, and to embrace your true self with courage and confidence. Trust in the journey of self-discovery and know that you have the strength and resilience to handle whatever challenges may come your way.

Throughout the year, the influence of Neptune in your 4th house of home and family will continue to bring a sense of spiritual connection and emotional sensitivity to your personal life. This is a time to cultivate a deeper sense of inner peace and contentment, to create a nurturing and supportive environment for yourself and your loved ones, and to trust in the power of intuition and imagination. Know that your home is your sanctuary, and that you have the ability to create a life of beauty, meaning, and purpose.

Overall, 2025 is a year of growth, adventure, and self-discovery for Sagittarius. With Jupiter bringing opportunities for learning and expansion, and with Mars and the eclipses bringing powerful energy for personal achievement and transformation, this is a time to embrace your unique path and purpose with enthusiasm and optimism. Trust in the journey, stay true to your values and ideals, and know that the universe is guiding you towards your highest potential. With an open heart and a adventurous spirit, you have the power to create a life of boundless joy, freedom, and fulfillment.

January 2025

Overview Horoscope for the Month:

Sagittarius, get ready for an exhilarating start to 2025! January is brimming with opportunities for growth, adventure, and self-discovery. As the month begins, Mars, the planet of action and energy, is retrograde in your 8th house of transformation and shared resources. This cosmic influence may bring up deep-seated fears or blockages around intimacy, vulnerability, and financial matters. However, don't let this discourage you – it's an opportunity to face your shadows head-on and emerge stronger, wiser, and more empowered.

The Full Moon in Cancer on January 13th illuminates your 8th house, bringing emotional intensity and the potential for profound healing and release. Trust your intuition, express your feelings openly, and allow yourself to be vulnerable with those you trust. This is a time to let go of past wounds, toxic patterns, or unhealthy attachments, and to create space for new levels of intimacy and connection.

Love:

Single Sagittarians may find themselves drawn to people who challenge them to grow and evolve, both emotionally and spiritually. Look for partners who appreciate your adventurous spirit and philosophical nature, but who also encourage you to explore your depths and face your fears. If you're already in a committed relationship, use this month's energies to deepen your bond through honest communication, shared adventures, and emotional vulnerability.

Venus, the planet of love and relationships, spends most of January in freedom-loving Aquarius, activating your 3rd house of communication and learning. This is a wonderful time to express your feelings through writing, art, or creative pursuits, and to engage in stimulating conversations with your partner or love interest. Attend a workshop, take a class, or plan a weekend getaway that feeds your mutual curiosity and desire for knowledge.

Career:

With Mars retrograde in your 8th house, you may feel a temporary slowdown or setback in your career or financial matters. Don't let this discourage you – use this time to reassess your goals, values, and motivations, and to make sure that your work aligns with your deepest passions and purpose. If you're feeling stuck or unfulfilled in your current job, start exploring new opportunities or ways to bring more creativity and meaning to your work.

The New Moon in Aquarius on January 29th activates your 3rd house of communication and learning, making it an excellent time to network, pitch ideas, or start a new course of study. Trust your innovative ideas and unique perspective, and don't be afraid to think outside the box or take calculated risks. Your natural optimism and enthusiasm will attract supportive people and opportunities your way.

Finances:

With Mars retrograde in your 8th house of shared resources, you may need to reassess your financial partnerships, investments, or debts. Be cautious about taking on new financial obligations or making impulsive decisions, and take the time to review your budget, savings, and long-term goals. If you're feeling stressed or overwhelmed about money matters, seek the guidance of a trusted financial advisor or mentor.

The Full Moon in Cancer on January 13th may bring a financial matter to a head, requiring you to confront any fears or insecurities around abundance and security. Trust that you have the resilience and resourcefulness to overcome any challenges, and focus on cultivating a mindset of gratitude, faith, and positive expectation. Remember that true wealth comes from within, and that you have the power to create the life and legacy you desire.

Health:

January's energies may bring a heightened awareness of your physical, emotional, and spiritual well-being. With Mars retrograde in your 8th house, you may be more sensitive to stress, anxiety, or hidden fears. Make sure to prioritize self-care, rest, and relaxation, and to create a daily routine that supports your overall health and vitality.

The Full Moon in Cancer on January 13th may bring up intense emotions or buried traumas that need to be acknowledged and released. Consider working with a therapist, healer, or spiritual guide to help you process any deep-seated issues or patterns that are holding you back. Trust in the power of vulnerability, forgiveness, and self-love to facilitate profound healing and transformation.

Travel:

With Venus in Aquarius activating your 3rd house of short trips and local adventures, January is a great month for exploring your own backyard or taking a spontaneous weekend getaway. Look for destinations that feed your curiosity, creativity, and desire for novelty, such as a quirky museum, art gallery, or cultural event.

If you're planning a longer trip or international adventure, be sure to do your research and take any necessary precautions, as Mars retrograde in your 8th house may bring unexpected delays, changes, or challenges. Stay flexible, open-minded, and trust that any detours or obstacles are ultimately leading you towards a greater purpose or life lesson.

Insights from the Stars:

Sagittarius, January 2025 is a month of deep soul-searching, emotional healing, and personal transformation. The cosmic energies are inviting you to confront your fears, embrace your shadows, and let go of anything that is no longer serving your highest good. Trust that the challenges you face are ultimately leading you towards a greater sense of freedom, authenticity, and purpose.

Remember that true growth and evolution often require discomfort, vulnerability, and the willingness to step outside your comfort zone. Embrace the journey with an open heart and a curious mind, and trust that the universe is conspiring in your favor, even when things feel uncertain or overwhelming.

Best Days of the Month:

- January 2nd: Venus enters Pisces, bringing a dreamy, romantic energy to your 4th house of home and family. Spend quality time with loved ones and create a cozy, nurturing space for yourself.
- January 6th: Mars retrograde re-enters Cancer, activating your 8th house of transformation and shared resources. Use this time to confront any fears or blockages around intimacy, vulnerability, and financial matters.
- January 13th: Full Moon in Cancer illuminates your 8th house, bringing emotional intensity and the potential for profound healing and release. Trust your intuition and allow yourself to be vulnerable with those you trust.
- January 18th: Mercury enters Aquarius, activating your 3rd house of communication and learning. Express your ideas and opinions with confidence, and seek out stimulating conversations and intellectual pursuits.
- January 29th: New Moon in Aquarius activates your 3rd house, making it an excellent time to network, pitch ideas, or

start a new course of study. Trust your innovative ideas and take calculated risks towards your goals.

February 2025

Overview Horoscope for the Month:

Sagittarius, February 2025 is a month of exciting opportunities, personal growth, and spiritual exploration. As the month begins, Venus, the planet of love and beauty, enters your 5th house of romance, creativity, and self-expression. This cosmic influence is set to bring joy, passion, and inspiration to your life, encouraging you to embrace your unique talents and follow your heart's desires.

The Full Moon in Leo on February 12th illuminates your 9th house of adventure, higher learning, and personal philosophy. This powerful lunar event may bring a culmination or turning point in your studies, travels, or spiritual pursuits. Trust your intuition, expand your horizons, and be open to new experiences and perspectives that challenge and inspire you.

Love:

With Venus gracing your 5th house of romance and pleasure, February is a fantastic month for love and relationships. If you're single, you may find yourself attracted to creative, passionate, and expressive individuals who share your zest for life. Be bold, flirtatious, and authentic in your interactions, and trust that your natural charisma and enthusiasm will attract the right people and opportunities your way.

If you're already in a committed relationship, use this month's energies to inject more fun, spontaneity, and romance into your connection. Plan a special date night, surprise your partner with a heartfelt gesture, or explore a new hobby or creative project together. The key is to prioritize joy, playfulness, and mutual appreciation, and to let your love light shine bright.

Career:

February's celestial influences are set to bring exciting opportunities and breakthroughs in your career and professional life. With Mars, the planet of action and ambition, entering your 10th house of career and public reputation on February 23rd, you may find yourself in the spotlight or taking on new leadership roles and responsibilities.

Trust your instincts, showcase your unique talents and skills, and don't be afraid to take calculated risks or pursue unconventional paths. Your natural optimism, enthusiasm, and visionary thinking will be your greatest assets, attracting supportive people and opportunities your way. Stay focused on your long-term goals, but also be open to unexpected detours or synchronicities that may lead you in a new and exciting direction.

Finances:

With Venus in your 5th house of creativity and self-expression, February is an excellent month to explore new ways to increase your income through your passions and talents. Consider starting a side hustle, freelancing, or monetizing a hobby or creative project that brings you joy and fulfillment.

At the same time, be mindful of impulsive spending or financial risk-taking, especially around the Full Moon in Leo on February 12th. Stay grounded in your values and long-term goals, and seek the guidance of a trusted financial advisor or mentor if needed. Remember that true abundance comes from within, and that your worth is not defined by your material possessions or bank balance.

Health:

February's energies are set to bring a renewed focus on your physical, mental, and emotional well-being. With the Sun and Mercury moving through your 4th house of home and family, you may find yourself craving more rest, relaxation, and nurturing self-care. Make sure to prioritize downtime, spend quality time with loved ones, and create a peaceful, supportive environment that allows you to recharge and rejuvenate.

At the same time, the Full Moon in Leo on February 12th may bring a burst of energy, vitality, and inspiration. Use this lunar influence to recommit to your fitness goals, try a new wellness practice, or explore a mind-body-spirit modality that aligns with your personal philosophy and beliefs. Trust that by taking care of yourself on all levels, you'll be better equipped to show up fully in all areas of your life.

Travel:

With the Full Moon in Leo illuminating your 9th house of travel and adventure, February is an excellent month for exploring new horizons and expanding your worldview. If possible, plan a trip or getaway that allows you to immerse yourself in a different culture, learn something new, or challenge your comfort zone.

If travel isn't feasible, consider exploring your own backyard or local community with fresh eyes and an open mind. Attend a cultural event, try a new cuisine, or strike up a conversation with someone from a different background or perspective. The key is to embrace curiosity, diversity, and the joy of discovery, and to let your adventurous spirit soar.

Insights from the Stars:

Sagittarius, February 2025 is a month of personal empowerment, creative expression, and spiritual growth. The cosmic energies are inviting you to embrace your unique gifts, follow your passions, and trust in the unfolding of your life's journey. Remember that you are the co-creator of your reality, and that your thoughts, beliefs, and actions have the power to shape your world.

Stay open to the magic and synchronicity of the universe, and trust that everything is happening for your highest good and evolution. Embrace the journey with a sense of wonder, gratitude, and faith, and know that you are exactly where you need to be, learning and growing in perfect divine timing.

Best Days of the Month:

- February 4th: Venus enters Aries, igniting your 5th house of romance, creativity, and self-expression. Embrace your passions, take bold risks, and let your unique light shine.
- February 12th: Full Moon in Leo illuminates your 9th house of adventure, higher learning, and personal philosophy.

Expand your horizons, seek new experiences, and trust your intuition.

- February 16th: Mercury enters Pisces, activating your 4th house of home and family. Spend quality time with loved ones, create a nurturing space, and prioritize rest and relaxation.
- February 18th: Sun enters Pisces, bringing a focus on your emotional and spiritual well-being. Practice self-care, connect with your inner wisdom, and trust the flow of life.
- February 23rd: Mars enters Leo, energizing your 10th house of career and public reputation. Take bold action towards your goals, showcase your talents, and embrace your leadership potential.

March 2025

Overview Horoscope for the Month:

Sagittarius, March 2025 is a month of profound transformation, spiritual awakening, and new beginnings. As the month begins, Saturn, the planet of structure, responsibility, and life lessons, enters your 5th house of romance, creativity, and self-expression. This significant cosmic shift may bring a more serious, committed energy to your love life and creative pursuits, asking you to take a mature, realistic approach to your passions and desires.

The New Moon in Aries on March 29th falls in your 5th house, signaling a powerful opportunity to set intentions and plant seeds for new creative projects, romantic adventures, or personal growth. Trust your instincts, take bold action, and believe in your ability to manifest your dreams into reality.

Love:

With Saturn now in your 5th house of romance and pleasure, March is a month of deepening commitment, emotional maturity, and long-term vision in your love life. If you're single, you may find yourself attracted to people who are stable, responsible, and share your values and goals. Take your time getting to know potential partners, and don't be afraid to set clear boundaries and expectations in your interactions.

If you're already in a committed relationship, use this month's energies to strengthen your bond through open communication, shared responsibilities, and a focus on building a solid foundation for the future. You may need to have some serious conversations about your goals, dreams, and long-term compatibility, but trust that this process will ultimately bring you closer together and deepen your love and respect for one another.

Career:

March's celestial influences are set to bring significant changes and opportunities in your career and professional life. With Pluto, the planet of power, transformation, and rebirth, entering your 2nd house of money and resources on March 23rd, you may find yourself reevaluating your financial goals, values, and priorities.

This is a time to let go of any limiting beliefs or patterns around money and success, and to embrace a more empowered, abundant mindset. Trust your skills, talents, and unique perspective, and don't be afraid to take calculated risks or pursue unconventional paths. Remember that true wealth comes from living in alignment with your authentic self and purpose, and that you have the power to create the life and career you desire.

Finances:

With Pluto now in your 2nd house of money and resources, March is an excellent month to take a deep dive into your financial situation and make any necessary changes or adjustments. This is a time to get clear on your values and priorities, and to create a budget and financial plan that supports your long-term goals and dreams.

You may also find yourself attracted to new sources of income or investment opportunities that align with your passions and purpose. Trust your instincts, do your research, and seek the guidance of a trusted financial advisor or mentor if needed. Remember that true abundance comes from a mindset of gratitude, generosity, and faith, and that your worth is not defined by your material possessions or bank balance.

Health:

March's energies are set to bring a renewed focus on your physical, mental, and emotional well-being.

With the Full Moon in Virgo on March 14th illuminating your 10th house of career and public reputation, you may find yourself feeling the effects of stress, overwork, or burnout. Make sure to prioritize self-care, rest, and relaxation, and to set clear boundaries around your time and energy.

At the same time, the New Moon in Aries on March 29th brings a powerful opportunity to recommit to your health and fitness goals. Use this lunar influence to start a new wellness practice, try a new form of exercise, or make positive changes to your diet and lifestyle. Trust that by taking care of yourself on all levels, you'll be better equipped to show up fully in all areas of your life.

Travel:

With Saturn now in your 5th house of adventure and exploration, March is an excellent month for planning a meaningful, purposeful trip or journey. Consider destinations that allow you to learn something new, challenge your comfort zone, or deepen your spiritual practice.

If travel isn't feasible, consider exploring your own backyard or local community with a fresh perspective and an open mind. Attend a workshop or retreat, volunteer for a cause you believe in, or connect with people from different cultures and backgrounds. The key is to embrace growth, learning, and the joy of discovery, and to let your adventurous spirit guide you towards new horizons.

Insights from the Stars:

Sagittarius, March 2025 is a month of profound transformation, personal growth, and spiritual awakening. The cosmic energies are inviting you to take a deep, honest look at your life, your relationships, and your path forward. Trust that the challenges and changes you face are ultimately leading you towards a more authentic, fulfilling, and purposeful existence.

Stay open to the wisdom and guidance of the universe, and trust that everything is happening for your highest good and evolution. Embrace the journey with a sense of curiosity, courage, and faith, and know that you have the strength, resilience, and inner resources to navigate any obstacles or setbacks that may arise.

Best Days of the Month:

- March 7th: Saturn enters Pisces, bringing a serious, committed energy to your 4th house of home and family. Focus on creating a stable, secure foundation for yourself and your loved ones.

- March 14th: Full Moon in Virgo illuminates your 10th house of career and public reputation. Celebrate your accomplishments, release any stress or burnout, and recommit to your professional goals and aspirations.
- March 20th: Sun enters Aries, igniting your 5th house of romance, creativity, and self-expression. Embrace your passions, take bold risks, and let your unique light shine.
- March 23rd: Pluto enters Aquarius, initiating a powerful transformation in your 2nd house of money and resources. Let go of limiting beliefs around abundance and success, and embrace a more empowered, abundant mindset.
- March 29th: New Moon in Aries falls in your 5th house of romance, creativity, and self-expression. Set intentions and plant seeds for new creative projects, romantic adventures, or personal growth. Trust your instincts and take bold action towards your dreams.

April 2025

Overview Horoscope for the Month:

Sagittarius, April 2025 is a month of exciting opportunities, personal growth, and spiritual exploration. As the month begins, Jupiter, your ruling planet, forms a square aspect to Pluto, signaling a time of deep transformation and soul-searching. This cosmic influence may bring up hidden fears, desires, or patterns that need to be acknowledged and released, paving the way for a more authentic, empowered version of yourself to emerge.

The New Moon in Aries on April 27th falls in your 5th house of romance, creativity, and self-expression, bringing a powerful opportunity to set intentions and plant seeds for new creative projects, romantic adventures, or personal growth. Trust your instincts, take bold action, and believe in your ability to manifest your dreams into reality.

Love:

With Venus, the planet of love and relationships, moving through your 5th house of romance and pleasure for most of April, this is a month of passion, creativity, and self-expression in your love life. If you're single, you may find yourself attracted to people who share your sense of adventure, humor, and zest for life. Be bold, flirtatious, and authentic in your interactions, and trust that your natural charisma and enthusiasm will attract the right people and opportunities your way.

If you're already in a committed relationship, use this month's energies to inject more fun, spontaneity, and romance into your connection. Plan a surprise date, express your love and appreciation in creative ways, or explore a new hobby or activity together. The key is to prioritize joy, playfulness, and mutual growth, and to let your love light shine bright.

Career:

April's celestial influences are set to bring exciting opportunities and breakthroughs in your career and professional life. With Mars, the planet of action and ambition, moving through your 10th house of career and public reputation, you may find yourself taking on new leadership roles, pursuing ambitious goals, or receiving recognition for your hard work and talents.

At the same time, the square aspect between Jupiter and Pluto on April 17th may bring up power struggles, conflicts, or challenges in your work environment. Stay true to your values and integrity, and don't be afraid to speak up for yourself or advocate for what you believe in. Trust that any obstacles or setbacks are ultimately leading you towards a more aligned, authentic path forward.

Finances:

With the North Node moving into your 8th house of shared resources and investments on April 11th, April is an excellent month to reevaluate your financial partnerships, debts, and long-term financial goals. This is a time to get clear on your values and priorities, and to make any necessary changes or adjustments to your budget, savings, or investment strategy.

You may also find yourself attracted to new sources of income or financial opportunities that align with your passions and purpose. Trust your instincts, do your research, and seek the guidance of a trusted financial advisor or mentor if needed. Remember that true abundance comes from a mindset of gratitude, generosity, and faith, and that your worth is not defined by your material possessions or bank balance.

Health:

April's energies are set to bring a renewed focus on your physical, mental, and emotional well-being. With the Sun moving through your 6th house of health and wellness for most of the month, this is an excellent time to prioritize self-care, establish healthy routines, and make positive changes to your diet, exercise, and lifestyle habits.

The Full Moon in Libra on April 12th illuminates your 11th house of friendships and social connections, reminding you of the importance of community, support, and connection in your overall well-being. Reach out to loved ones, participate in group activities or causes that inspire you, and surround yourself with people who uplift and encourage you to be your best self.

Travel:

With Saturn now in your 5th house of adventure and exploration, April is an excellent month for planning a meaningful, purposeful trip or journey. Consider destinations that allow you to learn something new, challenge your comfort zone, or deepen your spiritual practice.

If travel isn't feasible, consider exploring your own backyard or local community with a fresh perspective and an open mind. Attend a workshop or retreat, volunteer for a cause you believe in, or connect with people from different cultures and backgrounds. The key is to embrace growth, learning, and the joy of discovery, and to let your adventurous spirit guide you towards new horizons.

Insights from the Stars:

Sagittarius, April 2025 is a month of personal growth, spiritual exploration, and alignment with your true path and purpose. The cosmic energies are inviting you to let go of any limiting beliefs, fears, or patterns that may be holding you back from living your best life. Trust that the challenges and changes you face are ultimately leading you towards a more authentic, fulfilling, and joyful existence.

Stay open to the wisdom and guidance of the universe, and trust that everything is happening for your highest good and evolution. Embrace the journey with a sense of curiosity, courage, and faith, and know that you have the strength, resilience, and inner resources to navigate any obstacles or setbacks that may arise.

Best Days of the Month:

- April 4th: Saturn sextile Uranus brings a harmonious blend of stability and innovation to your life. Embrace change, take calculated risks, and trust in the power of your unique vision and perspective.

- April 11th: Venus enters Aries, igniting your 5th house of romance, creativity, and self-expression. Embrace your passions, take bold risks, and let your unique light shine.

- April 16th: Mercury enters Aries, enhancing your communication skills and mental agility. Express your ideas and opinions with confidence, and trust in the power of your voice and message.

- April 20th: Sun enters Taurus, bringing a grounded, practical energy to your 6th house of health and wellness. Focus on establishing healthy routines, nourishing your body and mind, and finding balance and stability in your daily life.

- April 27th: New Moon in Taurus falls in your 6th house of health and wellness. Set intentions and plant seeds for new healthy habits, self-care practices, or positive changes to your diet and lifestyle. Trust that small, consistent steps can lead to big, transformative results over time.

May 2025

Overview Horoscope for the Month:

Sagittarius, May 2025 is a month of powerful transformation, spiritual growth, and new beginnings. As the month begins, the North Node shifts into your 7th house of partnerships and relationships, signaling a time of significant growth and evolution in your connections with others. This cosmic influence may bring new people, opportunities, or challenges into your life that help you learn important lessons about love, collaboration, and compromise.

The New Moon in Taurus on May 26th falls in your 6th house of health, work, and daily routines, bringing a powerful opportunity to set intentions and make positive changes in these areas of your life. Trust your instincts, take practical steps towards your goals, and believe in your ability to create a more balanced, fulfilling, and productive existence.

Love:

With Venus, the planet of love and relationships, moving through your 7th house of partnerships for most of May, this is a month of deep connection, mutual growth, and shared purpose in your love life. If you're single, you may find yourself attracted to people who challenge you to grow, learn, and see things from a different perspective. Be open, honest, and authentic in your interactions, and trust that the right person will appreciate and value the real you.

If you're already in a committed relationship, use this month's energies to deepen your bond, communicate openly and honestly, and work together towards common goals and dreams. You may need to negotiate compromises, set clear boundaries, or address any imbalances or power struggles that arise. Remember that a healthy, loving relationship is built on a foundation of trust, respect, and mutual support.

Career:

May's celestial influences are set to bring exciting opportunities and breakthroughs in your career and professional life. With Mars, the planet of action and ambition, moving through your 10th house of career and public reputation until May 18th, you may find yourself taking on new challenges, pursuing ambitious goals, or receiving recognition for your hard work and talents.

At the same time, the North Node's shift into your 7th house of partnerships on May 11th may bring new collaborations, alliances, or mentors into your professional life. Be open to learning from others, sharing your skills and knowledge, and working together towards a common vision or purpose. Trust that the right people and opportunities will come into your life at the perfect time.

Finances:

With Jupiter, your ruling planet, forming a sextile aspect to Chiron in your 5th house of creativity and self-expression on May 18th, May is an excellent month to explore new ways to generate income or abundance through your unique talents and passions. This is a time to believe in yourself, take calculated risks, and trust in the power of your creative vision and entrepreneurial spirit.

At the same time, be mindful of any financial decisions or investments that seem too good to be true, especially around the time of the Full Moon in Scorpio on May 12th. Stay grounded in your values and long-term goals, and seek the guidance of a trusted financial advisor or mentor if needed. Remember that true wealth comes from living in alignment with your authentic self and purpose.

Health:

May's energies are set to bring a renewed focus on your physical, mental, and emotional well-being. With the Sun moving through your 6th house of health and wellness for most of the month, this is an excellent time to prioritize self-care, establish healthy routines, and make positive changes to your diet, exercise, and lifestyle habits.

The New Moon in Taurus on May 26th brings a powerful opportunity to set intentions and make a fresh start in these areas of your life. Consider trying a new workout routine, exploring holistic healing modalities, or making small, sustainable changes to your daily habits and routines. Remember that true health and vitality come from a balance of mind, body, and spirit.

Travel:

With Saturn now in your 5th house of adventure and exploration, May is an excellent month for planning a meaningful, purposeful trip or journey. Consider destinations that allow you to learn something new, challenge your comfort zone, or deepen your spiritual practice.

If travel isn't feasible, consider exploring your own backyard or local community with a fresh perspective and an open mind. Attend a workshop or retreat, volunteer for a cause you believe in, or connect with people from different cultures and backgrounds. The key is to embrace growth, learning, and the joy of discovery, and to let your adventurous spirit guide you towards new horizons.

Insights from the Stars:

Sagittarius, May 2025 is a month of powerful transformation, spiritual growth, and alignment with your true path and purpose. The cosmic energies are inviting you to let go of any limiting beliefs, fears, or patterns that may be holding you back from living your best life. Trust that the challenges and changes you face are ultimately leading you towards a more authentic, fulfilling, and joyful existence.

Stay open to the wisdom and guidance of the universe, and trust that everything is happening for your highest good and evolution. Embrace the journey with a sense of curiosity, courage, and faith, and know that you have the strength, resilience, and inner resources to navigate any obstacles or setbacks that may arise.

Best Days of the Month:

- May 11th: The North Node shifts into your 7th house of partnerships and relationships, signaling a time of significant growth and evolution in your connections with others. Be open to new people, opportunities, or challenges that help you learn important lessons about love, collaboration, and compromise.

- May 18th: Jupiter sextile Chiron in your 5th house of creativity and self-expression brings opportunities for healing, growth, and abundance through your unique talents and passions. Believe in yourself, take calculated risks, and trust in the power of your creative vision and entrepreneurial spirit.

- May 20th: Sun enters Gemini, bringing a curious, adaptable energy to your 7th house of partnerships and relationships. Engage in open, honest communication with others, seek out new perspectives and ideas, and be willing to learn and grow together.

- May 24th: Saturn enters Aries, bringing a serious, committed energy to your 5th house of creativity, self-expression, and romance. Take responsibility for your desires and passions, set clear goals and boundaries, and trust in the power of discipline and perseverance to manifest your dreams.

- May 26th: New Moon in Taurus falls in your 6th house of health, work, and daily routines. Set intentions and make positive changes in these areas of your life, focusing on practical steps, sustainable habits, and a holistic approach to well-being. Trust that small, consistent efforts can lead to big, transformative results over time.

June 2025

Overview Horoscope for the Month:

Sagittarius, June 2025 is a month of exciting adventures, personal growth, and spiritual exploration. As the month begins, Jupiter, your ruling planet, enters your 7th house of partnerships and relationships, bringing new opportunities for connection, collaboration, and shared purpose. This cosmic influence may bring significant people or experiences into your life that expand your horizons, challenge your beliefs, and help you grow in ways you never thought possible.

The Full Moon in Sagittarius on June 11th falls in your 1st house of self and identity, bringing a powerful opportunity to celebrate your unique talents, passions, and purpose. This is a time to let your light shine bright, express your authentic self, and trust in the power of your vision and wisdom to guide you towards your highest path and potential.

Love:

With Venus, the planet of love and relationships, moving through your 8th house of intimacy and transformation for most of June, this is a month of deep emotional connection, vulnerability, and spiritual growth in your love life. If you're single, you may find yourself attracted to people who challenge you to confront your fears, heal your wounds, and embrace your shadows. Be open, honest, and authentic in your interactions, and trust that the right person will appreciate and value the depth and complexity of your soul.

If you're already in a committed relationship, use this month's energies to deepen your bond, communicate openly and honestly about your desires and fears, and support each other through any challenges or changes that arise. You may need to let go of old patterns, beliefs, or dynamics that no longer serve your highest good, and trust in the transformative power of love to help you grow and evolve together.

Career:

June's celestial influences are set to bring exciting opportunities and breakthroughs in your career and professional life. With Mars, the planet of action and ambition, moving into your 10th house of career and public reputation on June 17th, you may find yourself taking on new responsibilities, pursuing ambitious goals, or receiving recognition for your hard work and talents.

At the same time, the North Node's presence in your 7th house of partnerships may bring new collaborations, alliances, or mentors into your professional life. Be open to learning from others, sharing your skills and knowledge, and working together towards a common vision or purpose. Trust that the right people and opportunities will come into your life at the perfect time to help you achieve your dreams and goals.

Finances:

With Neptune, the planet of dreams and intuition, forming a conjunction with the North Node in your 7th house of partnerships on June 7th, June is an excellent month to explore new ways to generate income or abundance through collaboration, creativity, and spiritual alignment. This is a time to trust your intuition, follow your heart, and believe in the power of your unique vision and purpose to attract the resources and support you need.

At the same time, be mindful of any financial decisions or investments that seem too good to be true, especially around the time of the New Moon in Gemini on June 25th. Stay grounded in your values and long-term goals, and seek the guidance of a trusted financial advisor or mentor if needed. Remember that true wealth comes from living in alignment with your authentic self and purpose, and that abundance flows when you trust in the universe to provide for your needs.

Health:

June's energies are set to bring a renewed focus on your physical, mental, and emotional well-being. With the Sun moving through your 7th house of relationships for most of the month, this is an excellent time to prioritize self-care, establish healthy boundaries, and cultivate supportive, nurturing connections with others.

The Full Moon in Sagittarius on June 11th brings a powerful opportunity to release any stress, tension, or negative habits that may be holding you back from optimal health and vitality. Consider trying a new wellness practice, such as yoga, meditation, or energy healing, or making small, sustainable changes to your diet and lifestyle. Remember that true health and happiness come from a balance of mind, body, and spirit, and that self-love is the foundation of all healing and growth.

Travel:

With Jupiter, your ruling planet, now in your 7th house of partnerships and relationships, June is an excellent month for planning a meaningful, shared adventure or journey with someone you love and trust. Consider destinations that allow you to explore new cultures, expand your mind, or deepen your spiritual practice together.

If travel isn't feasible, consider exploring your own backyard or local community with a fresh perspective and an open heart. Attend a workshop or retreat, volunteer for a cause you believe in, or connect with people from different backgrounds and walks of life. The key is to embrace growth, learning, and the joy of discovery, and to let your adventurous spirit guide you towards new horizons and possibilities.

Insights from the Stars:

Sagittarius, June 2025 is a month of powerful transformation, spiritual growth, and alignment with your true path and purpose. The cosmic energies are inviting you to let go of any limiting beliefs, fears, or patterns that may be holding you back from living your best life. Trust that the challenges and changes you face are ultimately leading you towards a more authentic, fulfilling, and joyful existence.

Stay open to the wisdom and guidance of the universe, and trust that everything is happening for your highest good and evolution. Embrace the journey with a sense of curiosity, courage, and faith, and know that you have the strength, resilience, and inner resources to navigate any obstacles or setbacks that may arise.

Best Days of the Month:

- June 4th: Pluto turns retrograde in your 3rd house of communication and learning, inviting you to reflect on your thoughts, beliefs, and perceptions. Be open to new ideas and perspectives, and trust in the power of your mind to create your reality.
- June 9th: Jupiter enters Cancer, bringing a nurturing, supportive energy to your 8th house of intimacy, transformation, and shared resources. Trust in the power of love, vulnerability, and emotional honesty to help you grow and evolve in your closest relationships.
- June 11th: Full Moon in Sagittarius falls in your 1st house of self and identity, bringing a powerful opportunity to celebrate your unique talents, passions, and purpose. Let your light shine bright, express your authentic self, and trust in the power of your vision and wisdom to guide you towards your highest path and potential.

- June 18th: Jupiter sextile Chiron in your 5th house of creativity, self-expression, and romance, bringing opportunities for healing, growth, and abundance through your unique talents and passions. Believe in yourself, take calculated risks, and trust in the power of your creative vision and entrepreneurial spirit.

- June 25th: New Moon in Cancer falls in your 8th house of intimacy, transformation, and shared resources. Set intentions and make positive changes in these areas of your life, focusing on emotional healing, vulnerability, and the power of love to transform and uplift. Trust that the universe is supporting you in letting go of what no longer serves you and embracing a more authentic, abundant life.

July 2025

Overview Horoscope for the Month:

Sagittarius, July 2025 is a month of personal growth, emotional healing, and spiritual awakening. As the month begins, Mars, the planet of action and ambition, enters your 9th house of adventure, higher learning, and personal philosophy. This cosmic influence may ignite a deep desire to explore new horizons, expand your mind, and discover your true purpose and path in life. Trust your intuition, follow your passions, and be open to unexpected opportunities and synchronicities that guide you towards your highest potential.

The Full Moon in Capricorn on July 10th falls in your 2nd house of values, finances, and self-worth, bringing a powerful opportunity to release any limiting beliefs or patterns around money and abundance. This is a time to align your resources and actions with your true values and priorities, and to trust in the universe to provide for your needs and desires. Believe in your own worth and value, and know that you are deserving of all the good things life has to offer.

Love:

With Venus, the planet of love and relationships, moving through your 9th house of adventure and expansion for most of July, this is a month of exciting romantic possibilities and spiritual growth in your love life. If you're single, you may find yourself attracted to people who share your love of learning, travel, and personal growth. Be open to meeting someone special while pursuing your passions or exploring new experiences, and trust that the right person will appreciate and support your adventurous spirit.

If you're already in a committed relationship, use this month's energies to deepen your connection through shared adventures, meaningful conversations, and spiritual practices. Plan a trip or retreat together, explore new ideas and philosophies, or simply make time to connect on a soul level. Remember that true love is a journey of growth, discovery, and mutual support, and that the challenges you face together can ultimately bring you closer and make your bond stronger.

Career:

July's celestial influences are set to bring exciting opportunities and breakthroughs in your career and professional life. With the Sun moving through your 8th house of transformation, power, and shared resources for most of the month, you may find yourself navigating complex dynamics or power struggles in your work environment. Trust your instincts, stand up for your values and beliefs, and be willing to let go of any situations or relationships that no longer serve your highest good.

At the same time, the New Moon in Leo on July 24th brings a powerful opportunity to set intentions and make a fresh start in your career and public image. Consider ways to showcase your unique talents and abilities, take on new leadership roles, or pursue a path that aligns with your true passions and purpose. Trust that your hard work and dedication will pay off, and that the universe is supporting you in manifesting your dreams and goals.

Finances:

With the Full Moon in Capricorn on July 10th falling in your 2nd house of values, finances, and self-worth, July is an excellent month to release any limiting beliefs or patterns around money and abundance. This is a time to get clear on your true values and priorities, and to align your resources and actions with what truly matters to you.

Consider creating a budget or financial plan that reflects your long-term goals and dreams, and be open to new sources of income or opportunities that align with your passions and purpose. Trust that the universe is always providing for your needs, and that abundance flows when you live in alignment with your authentic self and values.

Health:

July's energies are set to bring a renewed focus on your physical, mental, and emotional well-being. With Chiron, the wounded healer, moving through your 5th house of self-expression and creativity, this is an excellent time to explore holistic healing modalities that help you release past traumas, reconnect with your inner child, and express your true self.

Consider trying a new form of creative expression, such as art therapy, dance, or music, or engaging in activities that bring you joy and help you relax and recharge. Remember that true health and happiness come from a balance of mind, body, and spirit, and that self-love and self-care are essential for your overall well-being.

Travel:

With Mars now in your 9th house of adventure and exploration, July is an excellent month for planning a meaningful, transformative journey or experience. Consider destinations that allow you to immerse yourself in new cultures, learn something new, or challenge your comfort zone in a way that helps you grow and evolve.

If travel isn't feasible, consider exploring your own backyard or local community with a fresh perspective and an open mind. Attend a workshop or retreat, take a class or course that interests you, or connect with people from different backgrounds and walks of life. The key is to embrace growth, learning, and the joy of discovery, and to let your adventurous spirit guide you towards new horizons and possibilities.

Insights from the Stars:

Sagittarius, July 2025 is a month of powerful transformation, spiritual growth, and alignment with your true path and purpose. The cosmic energies are inviting you to let go of any limiting beliefs, fears, or patterns that may be holding you back from living your best life. Trust that the challenges and changes you face are ultimately leading you towards a more authentic, fulfilling, and joyful existence.

Stay open to the wisdom and guidance of the universe, and trust that everything is happening for your highest good and evolution. Embrace the journey with a sense of curiosity, courage, and faith, and know that you have the strength, resilience, and inner resources to navigate any obstacles or setbacks that may arise.

Best Days of the Month:

- July 1st: Mars enters Leo, bringing a bold, confident energy to your 9th house of adventure, higher learning, and personal philosophy. Trust your instincts, follow your passions, and be open to unexpected opportunities and synchronicities that guide you towards your highest potential.
- July 10th: Full Moon in Capricorn falls in your 2nd house of values, finances, and self-worth, bringing a powerful opportunity to release any limiting beliefs or patterns around money and abundance. Align your resources and actions with your true values and priorities, and trust in the universe to provide for your needs and desires.
- July 18th: Jupiter sextile Chiron in your 5th house of creativity, self-expression, and romance, bringing opportunities for healing, growth, and abundance through your unique talents and passions. Believe in yourself, take calculated risks, and trust in

the power of your creative vision and entrepreneurial spirit.

- July 22nd: Sun enters Leo, bringing a confident, expressive energy to your 9th house of adventure, higher learning, and personal philosophy. Let your light shine bright, express your authentic self, and trust in the power of your vision and wisdom to guide you towards your highest path and potential.

- July 24th: New Moon in Leo falls in your 9th house of adventure, higher learning, and personal philosophy. Set intentions and make positive changes in these areas of your life, focusing on personal growth, spiritual exploration, and the pursuit of your passions and dreams. Trust that the universe is supporting you in expanding your horizons and discovering your true purpose and path..

August 2025

Overview Horoscope for the Month:

Sagittarius, August 2025 is a month of deep introspection, emotional healing, and spiritual growth. As the month begins, Venus, the planet of love and relationships, enters your 10th house of career and public image, bringing opportunities for recognition, advancement, and harmonious connections in your professional life. At the same time, Mercury, the planet of communication and learning, goes retrograde in your 9th house of higher education, travel, and philosophy, inviting you to reflect on your beliefs, aspirations, and life direction.

The Full Moon in Aquarius on August 9th illuminates your 3rd house of communication, learning, and short trips, highlighting the need for open-mindedness, adaptability, and mental stimulation. Embrace your curiosity, seek out new ideas and perspectives, and trust in the power of your mind to expand your understanding of yourself and the world around you.

Love:

With Venus gracing your 10th house of career and public image for most of August, you may find your love life intertwined with your professional pursuits. If you're single, you may meet someone special through work or networking events, or find yourself attracted to someone who shares your ambitions and goals. Be open to unexpected connections and opportunities, but also be discerning about mixing business with pleasure.

If you're in a committed relationship, this month's energies can bring a renewed sense of purpose and partnership to your love life. Support each other's career aspirations, celebrate each other's successes, and find ways to balance your personal and professional responsibilities. Remember that true love is about growing and evolving together, and that the challenges you face can ultimately strengthen your bond and deepen your connection.

Career:

August's celestial influences are set to bring exciting opportunities and breakthroughs in your career and public life. With Venus in your 10th house and Jupiter, your ruling planet, in your 8th house of shared resources and power dynamics, you may find yourself negotiating important contracts, collaborations, or financial arrangements that can have a significant impact on your long-term success and security.

Trust your instincts, stand up for your values and beliefs, and be willing to take calculated risks to advance your goals and dreams. At the same time, be mindful of any power struggles or conflicts that may arise, and strive to maintain your integrity and professionalism in all your interactions. Remember that true success comes from alignment with your authentic self and purpose, and that the universe is supporting you in manifesting your highest potential.

Finances:

With the Sun moving through your 9th house of higher education, travel, and personal growth for most of August, this is an excellent time to invest in your own learning and development. Consider taking a course, attending a workshop or seminar, or pursuing a certification or degree that can enhance your skills and knowledge in your field.

At the same time, be mindful of any financial decisions or investments that may be influenced by Mercury's retrograde in your 9th house. Do your research, read the fine print, and seek the guidance of trusted advisors before committing to any long-term plans or agreements. Trust that the universe will provide for your needs and desires when you align your actions with your values and purpose.

Health:

August's energies are set to bring a renewed focus on your physical, mental, and emotional well-being. With Chiron, the wounded healer, moving through your 5th house of self-expression, creativity, and joy, this is an excellent time to explore holistic healing modalities that help you reconnect with your inner child, release past traumas, and express your authentic self.

Consider trying a new form of creative expression, such as art therapy, dance, or music, or engaging in activities that bring you pleasure and help you relax and recharge. At the same time, be mindful of any tendencies towards overindulgence or escapism, and strive to maintain a healthy balance of work and play, discipline and spontaneity. Remember that true health and happiness come from a wholistic approach to self-care and self-love.

Travel:

With Mercury retrograde in your 9th house of travel, higher education, and personal growth for most of August, this may not be the best time for long-distance trips or international adventures. If you do need to travel, be prepared for delays, cancellations, or unexpected changes in plans, and have a flexible mindset and backup options.

Instead, consider exploring your own backyard or local community with fresh eyes and an open mind. Take a day trip to a nearby town or attraction, attend a cultural event or festival, or simply spend time in nature, reconnecting with the beauty and wonder of the world around you. Remember that true adventure and growth can happen anywhere, anytime, when you approach life with curiosity, enthusiasm, and a willingness to learn and explore.

Insights from the Stars:

Sagittarius, August 2025 is a month of deep introspection, emotional healing, and spiritual growth. The cosmic energies are inviting you to reflect on your beliefs, aspirations, and life direction, and to make any necessary adjustments or course corrections to align with your authentic self and purpose.

Trust that the challenges and changes you face are ultimately leading you towards a more fulfilling, meaningful, and joyful existence. Stay open to the wisdom and guidance of the universe, and know that you have the strength, resilience, and inner resources to navigate any obstacles or setbacks that may arise.

Remember that true success and happiness come from living in alignment with your values, passions, and purpose, and that the journey of growth and self-discovery is an ongoing adventure.

Best Days of the Month:

- August 1st: Venus enters Virgo, bringing a practical, purposeful energy to your 10th house of career and public image. Focus on your long-term goals, attend to the details, and strive for excellence and efficiency in your professional pursuits.
- August 9th: Full Moon in Aquarius illuminates your 3rd house of communication, learning, and short trips. Embrace your curiosity, seek out new ideas and perspectives, and trust in the power of your mind to expand your understanding of yourself and the world around you.
- August 22nd: Sun enters Virgo, bringing a focused, analytical energy to your 10th house of career and public image. Set realistic goals, break them down into manageable steps, and take consistent action towards your aspirations and dreams.

- August 23rd: New Moon in Virgo falls in your 10th house of career and public image, bringing a powerful opportunity to set intentions and make a fresh start in your professional life. Clarify your vision, align your actions with your values and purpose, and trust in the universe to support you in manifesting your highest potential.

- August 28th: Venus trines Neptune in your 4th house of home, family, and emotional security, bringing a dreamy, romantic energy to your personal life. Connect with loved ones, create a nurturing and inspiring environment, and trust in the power of love, compassion, and creativity to heal and transform your relationships and your sense of belonging.

September 2025

Overview Horoscope for the Month:

Sagittarius, September 2025 is a month of new beginnings, personal growth, and spiritual awakening. As the month starts, Mars, the planet of action and ambition, enters your 11th house of friendships, community, and social activism. This cosmic influence may inspire you to connect with like-minded individuals, join a cause or movement that aligns with your values, or take on a leadership role in your social circle. Trust your instincts, follow your passions, and be open to collaboration and teamwork as you pursue your goals and dreams.

The Full Moon in Pisces on September 7th brings a powerful opportunity for emotional healing, forgiveness, and release. Falling in your 4th house of home, family, and emotional foundations, this lunation invites you to let go of any past wounds, resentments, or limiting patterns that may be holding you back from experiencing true intimacy, security, and belonging. Practice self-compassion, seek support from loved ones, and trust in the power of love and acceptance to transform your relationships and your sense of self.

Love:

With Venus, the planet of love and relationships, moving through your 11th house of friendships and community for most of September, you may find your love life intertwined with your social life and group activities. If you're single, you may meet someone special through a shared interest, hobby, or cause, or find yourself attracted to someone who shares your ideals and vision for the future. Be open to unconventional connections and unexpected opportunities, but also be discerning about who you let into your inner circle.

If you're in a committed relationship, this month's energies can bring a renewed sense of shared purpose and partnership to your love life. Work together towards a common goal, support each other's individuality and independence, and find ways to balance your personal and social responsibilities. Remember that true love is about acceptance, understanding, and growth, and that the challenges you face can ultimately strengthen your bond and deepen your connection.

Career:

September's celestial influences are set to bring exciting opportunities and breakthroughs in your career and professional life. With the Sun moving through your 10th house of career, reputation, and public image for most of the month, you may find yourself in the spotlight or taking on new roles and responsibilities that showcase your unique talents and abilities.

At the same time, Mercury, the planet of communication and learning, moves into your 11th house of networking and social connections on September 18th, highlighting the importance of building and maintaining professional relationships. Attend industry events, join a professional organization, or reach out to colleagues and mentors for advice and support. Remember that true success comes from collaboration, innovation, and a willingness to learn and grow.

Finances:

With the New Moon in Virgo on September 21st falling in your 10th house of career and public recognition, this is an excellent time to set intentions and make plans for your long-term financial goals and aspirations. Consider ways to increase your income, invest in your skills and education, or pursue a promotion or raise that reflects your value and contributions.

At the same time, be mindful of any tendencies towards overspending or financial risk-taking, especially around the time of the Full Moon in Pisces on September 7th. Practice gratitude for what you already have, focus on experiences rather than possessions, and trust that the universe will provide for your needs and desires when you align your actions with your values and purpose.

Health:

September's energies are set to bring a renewed focus on your physical, mental, and emotional well-being. With Chiron, the wounded healer, moving through your 5th house of self-expression, creativity, and joy, this is an excellent time to explore holistic healing modalities that help you reconnect with your inner child, release past traumas, and express your authentic self.

Consider trying a new form of creative expression, such as art therapy, dance, or music, or engaging in activities that bring you pleasure and help you relax and recharge. At the same time, be mindful of any tendencies towards overindulgence or escapism, and strive to maintain a healthy balance of work and play, discipline and spontaneity. Remember that true health and happiness come from a wholistic approach to self-care and self-love.

Travel:

With Jupiter, your ruling planet, now direct in your 9th house of travel, higher education, and personal growth, September is an excellent month for planning a meaningful, transformative journey or experience. Consider destinations that allow you to immerse yourself in new cultures, learn something new, or challenge your comfort zone in a way that helps you grow and evolve.

If travel isn't feasible, consider exploring your own backyard or local community with a fresh perspective and an open mind. Attend a workshop or retreat, take a class or course that interests you, or connect with people from different backgrounds and walks of life. The key is to embrace growth, learning, and the joy of discovery, and to let your adventurous spirit guide you towards new horizons and possibilities.

Insights from the Stars:

Sagittarius, September 2025 is a month of powerful transformation, spiritual growth, and alignment with your true path and purpose. The cosmic energies are inviting you to let go of any limiting beliefs, fears, or patterns that may be holding you back from living your best life. Trust that the challenges and changes you face are ultimately leading you towards a more authentic, fulfilling, and joyful existence.

Stay open to the wisdom and guidance of the universe, and trust that everything is happening for your highest good and evolution. Embrace the journey with a sense of curiosity, courage, and faith, and know that you have the strength, resilience, and inner resources to navigate any obstacles or setbacks that may arise.

Best Days of the Month:

- September 7th: Full Moon in Pisces illuminates your 4th house of home, family, and emotional foundations. Release past wounds and practice self-compassion.
- September 18th: Mercury enters Libra, activating your 11th house of friendships, networking, and social connections. Build and maintain professional relationships.
- September 21st: New Moon in Virgo falls in your 10th house of career and public recognition. Set intentions for your long-term financial goals and aspirations.

- September 22nd: Sun enters Libra, bringing a harmonious, balanced energy to your 11th house of friendships, community, and social activism. Connect with like-minded individuals and pursue your passions.
- September 29th: Venus trines Saturn in your 3rd house of communication and learning, bringing a stabilizing, committed energy to your relationships and interactions. Have important conversations and make long-term plans.

October 2025

Overview Horoscope for the Month:

Sagittarius, October 2025 is a month of deep introspection, emotional healing, and spiritual growth. As the month begins, Venus, the planet of love and relationships, enters your 12th house of spirituality, solitude, and inner work. This cosmic influence invites you to retreat from the world, reflect on your values and beliefs, and connect with your inner wisdom and intuition. Trust the process of letting go, surrendering control, and allowing yourself to be guided by a higher power or purpose.

The Full Moon in Aries on October 6th illuminates your 5th house of romance, creativity, and self-expression, bringing a powerful opportunity to express your authentic self, pursue your passions, and let your light shine. Take a risk, follow your heart, and trust in the power of your unique talents and abilities to bring joy, inspiration, and meaning to your life and the lives of others.

Love:

With Venus moving through your 12th house of spirituality and inner work for most of October, your love life may take on a more introspective, intuitive, and unconditional quality. If you're single, you may find yourself attracted to someone who shares your spiritual values and beliefs, or who helps you connect with your higher self and purpose. Be open to the unexpected, trust your intuition, and allow yourself to be vulnerable and authentic in your interactions.

If you're in a committed relationship, this month's energies can bring a deeper level of intimacy, compassion, and unconditional love to your partnership. Practice forgiveness, let go of any past wounds or resentments, and focus on the present moment and the love that you share. Remember that true love is a spiritual journey of growth, healing, and self-discovery, and that the challenges you face can ultimately bring you closer to your authentic self and to each other.

Career:

October's celestial influences are set to bring exciting opportunities and breakthroughs in your career and professional life. With Mars, the planet of action and ambition, moving through your 10th house of career, reputation, and public image for most of the month, you may find yourself taking on new challenges, pursuing your goals with passion and determination, and making significant progress towards your long-term aspirations.

At the same time, the New Moon in Libra on October 21st falls in your 11th house of networking, community, and social connections, highlighting the importance of collaboration, teamwork, and shared values in your professional life. Seek out like-minded individuals and organizations that align with your vision and purpose, and be open to new ideas and perspectives that can help you grow and succeed. Remember that true success comes from being true to yourself and making a positive impact on the world around you.

Finances:

With Pluto, the planet of power, transformation, and rebirth, now direct in your 2nd house of money, resources, and self-worth, October is an excellent month for making positive changes and breakthroughs in your financial life. Consider ways to increase your income, invest in your skills and education, or pursue new opportunities that align with your values and passions.

At the same time, be mindful of any tendencies towards obsession, control, or power struggles around money and resources, especially around the time of the Full Moon in Aries on October 6th. Practice gratitude for what you already have, focus on experiences rather than possessions, and trust that the universe will provide for your needs and desires when you align your actions with your higher purpose and soul's calling.

Health:

October's energies are set to bring a renewed focus on your physical, mental, and emotional well-being. With the Sun moving through your 12th house of spirituality, solitude, and inner work for most of the month, this is an excellent time to prioritize self-care, rest, and relaxation, and to explore holistic healing modalities that help you connect with your inner wisdom and intuition.

Consider trying a new form of meditation, yoga, or energy healing, or engaging in activities that bring you peace, clarity, and inner calm. At the same time, be mindful of any tendencies towards escapism, addiction, or self-sabotage, and strive to maintain a healthy balance of introspection and action, solitude and connection. Remember that true health and happiness come from a wholistic approach to self-care and self-love, and that your inner world is just as important as your outer world.

Travel:

With Jupiter, your ruling planet, now retrograde in your 8th house of transformation, power, and shared resources, October may not be the best month for long-distance travel or adventurous journeys. Instead, consider taking a more introspective, transformative approach to your travels, such as attending a spiritual retreat, exploring your ancestral roots, or delving into the mysteries of life and death.

If travel isn't possible or practical, consider exploring your own inner landscape through journaling, dream work, or creative visualization. Trust that the answers and insights you seek are already within you, and that the journey of self-discovery and spiritual growth is the most important journey of all.

Insights from the Stars:

Sagittarius, October 2025 is a month of deep introspection, emotional healing, and spiritual growth. The cosmic energies are inviting you to let go of any limiting beliefs, fears, or patterns that may be holding you back from living your best life, and to connect with your inner wisdom, intuition, and higher purpose.

Trust that the challenges and changes you face are ultimately leading you towards a more authentic, fulfilling, and joyful existence, and that the universe is conspiring in your favor, even when things feel uncertain or overwhelming. Stay open to the guidance and support of your angels, guides, and higher self, and know that you are never alone on this journey of growth and self-discovery.

Best Days of the Month:

- October 6th: Full Moon in Aries illuminates your 5th house of romance, creativity, and self-expression. Express your authentic self and pursue your passions.
- October 13th: Pluto turns direct in your 2nd house of money, resources, and self-worth. Make positive changes and breakthroughs in your financial life.
- October 21st: New Moon in Libra falls in your 11th house of networking, community, and social connections. Seek out like-minded individuals and organizations that align with your vision and purpose.
- October 22nd: Sun enters Scorpio, bringing a deep, transformative energy to your 12th house of spirituality, solitude, and inner work. Explore your inner landscape and connect with your higher self.

- October 29th: Mercury enters Sagittarius, activating your 1st house of self, identity, and personal goals. Communicate your ideas and aspirations with confidence and enthusiasm.

November 2025

Overview Horoscope for the Month:

Sagittarius, November 2025 is a month of deep introspection, spiritual growth, and new beginnings. As the month starts, the Sun is in your 12th house of spirituality, solitude, and inner work, inviting you to retreat from the world, reflect on your life, and connect with your inner wisdom and intuition. This is a time to let go of any past wounds, resentments, or limiting patterns, and to open yourself up to new possibilities, insights, and blessings.

The New Moon in Scorpio on November 20th falls in your 12th house, bringing a powerful opportunity to set intentions for your spiritual growth, emotional healing, and inner transformation. Trust the process of surrendering control, embracing change, and allowing yourself to be guided by a higher power or purpose.

Love:

With Venus, the planet of love and relationships, moving through your 1st house of self, identity, and personal goals for most of November, your love life is likely to be closely intertwined with your personal growth and self-discovery. If you're single, focus on loving and accepting yourself fully, cultivating a strong sense of self-worth and self-respect, and trusting that the right person will come into your life at the perfect time.

If you're in a relationship, use this month's energies to deepen your connection, communicate openly and honestly about your needs and desires, and support each other's individual journeys of growth and self-realization. Be willing to let go of any past hurts or resentments, and focus on creating a loving, compassionate, and authentic partnership.

Career:

November's celestial influences are set to bring exciting opportunities and breakthroughs in your career and professional life. With Mars, the planet of action and ambition, moving through your 11th house of networking, community, and social connections, focus on building and nurturing professional relationships, collaborating with like-minded individuals, and aligning your work with your values and vision for the future.

Trust your instincts, take calculated risks, and be open to new ideas and perspectives that can help you grow and succeed. At the same time, be mindful of any power struggles or conflicts that may arise, and strive to maintain your integrity and professionalism in all your interactions.

Finances:

With Jupiter, your ruling planet, now direct in your 8th house of transformation, power, and shared resources, November is an excellent month for making positive changes and breakthroughs in your financial life. Consider ways to increase your income, invest in your skills and education, or pursue new opportunities that align with your passions and purpose.

At the same time, be mindful of any tendencies towards overspending or financial risk-taking, especially around the time of the Full Moon in Taurus on November 5th. Practice gratitude for what you already have, focus on experiences rather than possessions, and trust that the universe will provide for your needs and desires when you align your actions with your values and intentions.

Health:

November's energies are set to bring a renewed focus on your physical, mental, and emotional well-being. With the Sun moving through your 12th house of spirituality, solitude, and inner work for most of the month, prioritize self-care, rest, and relaxation, and explore holistic healing modalities that help you connect with your inner wisdom and intuition.

Consider trying a new form of meditation, yoga, or energy healing, or engaging in activities that bring you peace, clarity, and inner calm. At the same time, be mindful of any tendencies towards escapism, addiction, or self-sabotage, and strive to maintain a healthy balance of introspection and action, solitude and connection.

Travel:

With the North Node now in your 6th house of work, health, and daily routines, November may be a good month for short trips or local adventures that help you break out of your comfort zone, explore new places and experiences, and gain fresh perspectives on your life and work.

Consider taking a day trip to a nearby town or natural wonder, attending a workshop or retreat that aligns with your interests and goals, or simply spending time in nature, reconnecting with the beauty and wisdom of the world around you. Trust your curiosity and sense of adventure, and be open to unexpected opportunities for growth and learning.

Insights from the Stars:

Sagittarius, November 2025 is a month of deep introspection, emotional healing, and spiritual growth. The cosmic energies are inviting you to let go of any limiting beliefs, fears, or patterns that may be holding you back from living your best life, and to connect with your inner wisdom, intuition, and higher purpose.

Trust that the challenges and changes you face are ultimately leading you towards a more authentic, fulfilling, and joyful existence, and that the universe is conspiring in your favor, even when things feel uncertain or overwhelming. Stay open to the guidance and support of your angels, guides, and higher self, and know that you are never alone on this journey of growth and self-discovery.

Best Days of the Month:

- November 5th: Full Moon in Taurus illuminates your 6th house of work, health, and daily routines. Release any stress, tension, or unhealthy habits, and embrace a more balanced, grounded approach to your well-being.
- November 7th: Venus enters Sagittarius, activating your 1st house of self, identity, and personal goals. Focus on self-love, self-

acceptance, and personal growth, and let your unique light shine brightly in the world.

- November 20th: New Moon in Scorpio falls in your 12th house of spirituality, solitude, and inner work. Set intentions for spiritual growth, emotional healing, and inner transformation, and trust the process of letting go and surrendering to a higher power.

- November 21st: Sun enters Sagittarius, bringing a confident, optimistic energy to your 1st house of self, identity, and personal goals. Celebrate your unique talents and qualities, pursue your passions and dreams, and embrace the adventure of life.

- November 28th: Mercury enters Sagittarius, enhancing your communication skills and mental agility. Express your ideas and opinions with clarity, enthusiasm, and conviction, and trust in the power of your voice and message to inspire and uplift others.

December 2025

Overview Horoscope for the Month:

Sagittarius, December 2025 is a month of celebration, reflection, and new beginnings. With the Sun in your sign for most of the month, you are likely to feel a renewed sense of energy, confidence, and enthusiasm for life. This is a time to embrace your unique talents and qualities, pursue your passions and goals, and let your light shine brightly in the world.

The New Moon in Sagittarius on December 19th brings a powerful opportunity to set intentions for the year ahead, clarify your vision and purpose, and take bold action towards your dreams. Trust your instincts, follow your heart, and believe in the power of your own potential and possibilities.

Love:

With Venus, the planet of love and relationships, moving through your 2nd house of values, resources, and self-worth for most of December, your love life is likely to be closely intertwined with your sense of security, stability, and personal values. If you're single, focus on building a strong foundation of self-love and self-respect, cultivating a sense of abundance and prosperity, and trusting that the right person will appreciate and value you for who you are.

If you're in a relationship, use this month's energies to deepen your commitment, express your love and appreciation through tangible actions and gestures, and create a shared vision for the future that aligns with both of your values and goals. Be willing to have honest conversations about money, resources, and long-term planning, and trust that your love can weather any challenges or changes that may arise.

Career:

December's celestial influences are set to bring exciting opportunities and breakthroughs in your career and professional life. With Mars, the planet of action and ambition, moving through your 12th house of spirituality, solitude, and inner work, focus on aligning your work with your higher purpose, trusting your intuition, and letting go of any limiting beliefs or patterns that may be holding you back from success and fulfillment.

Consider taking time for reflection, meditation, or journaling to gain clarity on your long-term goals and aspirations, and be open to unexpected insights or opportunities that may arise from your inner wisdom and guidance. At the same time, be mindful of any tendencies towards burnout, overwork, or self-sabotage, and strive to maintain a healthy balance of effort and ease, action and rest.

Finances:

With Jupiter, your ruling planet, now in your 9th house of travel, higher education, and personal growth, December is an excellent month for investing in your own learning and development, exploring new sources of income or wealth, and expanding your financial horizons.

Consider taking a course, attending a workshop or seminar, or pursuing a certification or degree that can enhance your skills and knowledge in your field. At the same time, be mindful of any tendencies towards overspending or financial risk-taking, especially around the time of the Full Moon in Gemini on December 4th. Stay grounded in your values and long-term goals, and trust that abundance flows when you align your actions with your authentic self and purpose.

Health:

December's energies are set to bring a renewed focus on your physical, mental, and emotional well-being. With the Sun in your sign for most of the month, prioritize self-care, joy, and vitality, and explore holistic healing modalities that help you feel your best and shine your brightest.

Consider trying a new form of exercise, such as dance, yoga, or martial arts, or making small, sustainable changes to your diet and lifestyle that support your overall health and happiness. At the same time, be mindful of any tendencies towards overindulgence or neglect, and strive to maintain a healthy balance of discipline and pleasure, effort and ease.

Travel:

With Mercury, the planet of communication and learning, moving through your 1st house of self, identity, and personal goals for most of December, this is an excellent month for short trips, local adventures, and intellectual pursuits that help you expand your mind, broaden your horizons, and gain new perspectives on yourself and the world around you.

Consider taking a weekend getaway to a nearby city or natural wonder, attending a cultural event or festival that sparks your curiosity and creativity, or simply spending time exploring your own neighborhood or community with fresh eyes and an open heart. Trust your sense of adventure and discovery, and be open to unexpected opportunities for growth, learning, and connection.

Insights from the Stars:

Sagittarius, December 2025 is a month of celebration, reflection, and new beginnings. The cosmic energies are inviting you to embrace your unique talents and qualities, pursue your passions and goals, and let your light shine brightly in the world.

Trust that you have the wisdom, courage, and resilience to navigate any challenges or changes that may arise, and that the universe is always supporting you on your path of growth and evolution. Stay open to the magic and synchronicity of life, and know that your dreams and desires are leading you towards your highest potential and purpose.

Best Days of the Month:

- December 4th: Full Moon in Gemini illuminates your 7th house of partnerships and relationships. Celebrate your connections, communicate openly and honestly, and find a balance between your individual needs and the needs of others.

- December 19th: New Moon in Sagittarius brings a powerful opportunity to set intentions for the year ahead, clarify your vision and purpose, and take bold action towards your dreams. Trust your instincts, follow your heart, and believe in the power of your own potential and possibilities.

- December 21st: Sun enters Capricorn, bringing a grounded, practical energy to your 2nd house of values, resources, and self-worth. Focus on building a strong foundation for your goals and dreams, and trust that your efforts will pay off in the long run.

- December 24th: Venus enters Capricorn, enhancing your sense of commitment, responsibility, and long-term planning in your relationships and financial life. Express your love and appreciation with tangible actions and gestures, and create a shared vision for the future that aligns with your values and goals.

- December 29th: Mercury enters Capricorn, sharpening your mind and communication skills in matters of business, career, and practical planning. Trust your intelligence and expertise, and communicate your ideas with clarity, confidence, and conviction.

Made in the USA
Las Vegas, NV
17 December 2024

14558322R00069